Intro

My grandfather, Victor Lloyd, loved quizzes and crossword puzzles and published many fine quiz books in the original Pillar Publishing Dublin in the 1930s and 40s.

Now that I have created Pillar International Publishing, I pay tribute to Granda Lloyd's enterprise with this small series of books.

In this particular book I have brought together some questions to challenge the cleverest of quizzers.

The format of the book is 5 quizzes of 10 rounds of 10 questions. I have also included 20 bonus tie-breaker questions.

The questions vary in difficulty from easy to not so easy

Enjoy!

Mark.

Direct any feedback or corrections to: info@indiepillar.com.

Quiz 1
Round 1

1) Who wrote 'Chitty Chitty Bang Bang'?
2) Who wrote the Artemis Fowl series?
3) Who invented basketball?
4) In astrology which sign is represented by a bull?
5) What is the longest river in Ireland?
6) Which German car manufacturer is associated with the 911, Cayenne and Boxter
7) Which Dickens book features Dothebys Hall?
8) What is the name given to a violent riot started to massacre an ethnic or religious group?
9) Who created the comic *Tin Tin*?
10) How many bytes in 1 kilobyte, in computer terminology?

Quiz 1
Round 2

1) What is the capital city of Hungary?
2) How many pockets does a Snooker table have?
3) According to Norse legend, after dying in battle a soldier goes to which hall?
4) In what year did World War One end?
5) Which T.S. Eliot poem features the famous 'not with a bang' line?
6) Who was the last Tsar of Russia?
7) Who composed *The Hallelujah Chorus*?
8) In Major League Baseball, if the first New York team is the Yankees, what is the second?
9) Kale, cabbage and broccoli are part of which plant genus?
10) Which rapper's birth name was Curtis Jackson?

Quiz 1
Round 3

1) Yehudi Menuhin was famously associated with which instrument?

2) In which country would you find the Cliffs of Moher?

3) Which word, used to describe feeling joy at someone's misery, has been taken into English from German?

4) What is the name of the fasting month in Islam?

5) Which member of *The Fast Show* cast wrote the Young James Bond series of books?

6) In the animated film *Kung Fu Panda*, who voiced Master Shifu?

7) Who directed *Jurassic Park* (1993)?

8) Dying in BC 71, what was the name of the slave leader who led a revolt against the Romans and would be portrayed by Kirk Douglas in film?

9) Which book's eponymous heroine fell in love with Mr. Rochester?

10) What country has the internet domain '.ca'?

Quiz 1

Round 4

1) In the UK, what was added to the town names of Beeston, Bognor and Lyme?

2) In golf, what is also known as a three strokes under par or a 'double eagle'?

3) What is the name given in India to elephant drivers?

4) In which U.S. city would you find the *Country Music Hall of Fame*?

5) Australia made a significant change to the $5 note in 2000 - what did they remove?

6) Fill in the blank in the NFL American Football team - The <blank> Eagles ...

7) Who wrote the book 'I know why the caged bird sings'?

8) What is the smallest organ of the human body?

9) Which classic British comedy features Del Boy and Rodney?

10) Who was the lead singer of *The Boomtown Rats*?

Quiz 1
Round 5

1) Who painted 'The Mona Lisa'?
2) Which country's flag features a cedar?
3) Which volcano erupted in AD79, destroying the town of Herculaneum?
4) Who wrote the book 'Northern Lights'?
5) What country's capital city is Bratislava?
6) Which island group's name comes from the Latin for the *Island of the Dogs*?
7) In which year was the first modern Olympics held?
8) With which religion would you associate The Koran?
9) On a Qwerty keyboard, what is the last letter on the second row of letters?
10) Who directed *Blade Runner* (1982)?

Quiz 1
Round 6

1) How old was Harry Potter when he entered Hogwarts?

2) In metres, how long is an Olympic swimming pool?

3) What cartoon family lives at *39 Stone Canyon Way*?

4) Which English football team plays at Anfield?

5) Who is the Greek goddess of love?

6) Which singer's birth name was Robert Zimmerman?

7) In bingo, what number is two fat ladies?

8) In astrology which sign is represented by a fish?

9) In 2000 who released the album *The Marshall Mathers LP*?

10) What fruit is traditionally used to make Kirsch?

Quiz 1
Round 7

1) Which MLB baseball team is based in Fenway Park?

2) In what mountain range is Mont Blanc?

3) Which Jewish holy day is also known as *The Day of Atonement*?

4) What was the surname of Truman, in the movie *The Truman Show*?

5) *Richard of York Gave Battle in Vain* is a mnemonic for what?

6) What is Claustrophobia a fear of?

7) Which classic comedy features three priests on Craggy Island?

8) How many points is a yellow ball worth in snooker?

9) In the 1960 film Psycho, what was the name of the motel?

10) Which famous general was killed at The Battle of the Little Bighorn?

Quiz 1

Round 8

1) Who was the first man in space?

2) In emails, what does BCC stand for?

3) Who composed *The Ride of the Valkyries*?

4) Who was the Russian Leader at the outbreak of WWII?

5) Which cartoon family lives at 744 Evergreen Terrace?

6) Which important political position has been held by Kurt Waldheim and Boutros Boutros Ghali?

7) Fill in the blank in the NFL American Football team - The Cleveland <blank> …

8) From what American Indian tribe was Geronimo?

9) Which automobile company makes the Prius?

10) Poland and Belgium share what national flower?

Quiz 1
Round 9

1) How is a Chinese gooseberry better known?

2) Which conference to decide the post-war division of Europe took place after the Tehran Conference and before the Potsdam conference?

3) Which writer's birth name was Samuel Longhorne Clemens?

4) What is the capital city of Liechtenstein?

5) What fruit are Concord, Conference and Beth types of?

6) What was the Allied code-name for the Battle of Normandy?

7) What famous drink is associated with St. James' Gate in Dublin, Ireland?

8) Which famous playwright married Marilyn Monroe?

9) Which playwright became the first president of the Czech Republic in 1993?

10) Which military organisation's motto is 'Legio Patria Nostra'?

Quiz 1
Round 10

1) Which Shakespeare play features Polonius?

2) From which type of flower do we get vanilla?

3) What do the letters *USB* stand for in electronics?

4) Which is the largest South American country?

5) What is the capital city of South Korea?

6) Who won the Best Actress Oscar in 2011 for *The Iron Lady*?

7) Who wrote 'Portrait of the Artist as a Young Man'?

8) How is Jorge Mario Bergoglio better known?

9) With which sport would you associate the nicknames Whirlwind and Hurricane?

10) Who was the U.K. Prime Minister at the outbreak of WWII?

Quiz 2

Round 1

1) What is the capital city of Singapore?

2) Which European country gave women the vote in 1986?

3) Which toy was invented by Ole Kirk Christiansen?

4) In which city were the first modern Olympics held?

5) Which desert's name is based on the Tswana word for 'great thirst'?

6) In photography, what does SLR mean?

7) In Norse mythology, who was the allfather of the Gods and ruler of Asgard?

8) What is the capital city of Croatia?

9) Who founded The Church of Scientology?

10) What are Braeburn, Golden Delicious and Pink Lady types of?

Quiz 2

Round 2

1) Who was granted the first telephone patent?

2) Who played Tonto in the 2013 film *The Lone Ranger*?

3) What chemical has the symbol He?

4) Which letter of the alphabet has more than one syllable?

5) Amarillo, on Route 66, gets its name from the Spanish for what colour?

6) In the atom, what are the positively charged particles called?

7) What is the state capital of Alaska?

8) In what city would you find Schiphol airport?

9) Who was the first man to walk on the moon?

10) What is the capital city of New Zealand?

Quiz 2
Round 3

1) What name was given to the Spanish and Portuguese explorer-soldiers from the fifteenth to seventeenth centuries?

2) In 2012, who won a Record of the Year Grammy with 'Rolling in the Deep'?

3) What name is derived from the Greek for 'terrible lizard'?

4) What in computers is RAM?

5) Which comedy duo starred in the British comedy series from 1990 to 1993 as Jeeves and Wooster?

6) In the U.S. it is called Saran Wrap - what is it called in the U.K.?

7) What is the first letter of the Greek alphabet?

8) In database programming, what does SQL stand for?

9) Fill in the blank in the NFL American Football team - The Green Bay <blank> …

10) 'Do not go gentle into that good night' was written by which poet?

Quiz 2

Round 4

1) Which word, used to describe an extensive array of food, has been taken into English from Swedish?

2) In what country was poet Pablo Neruda born?

3) What country do the French call Angleterre?

4) Which Shakespeare play features the Moor of Venice?

5) In Star Wars, what was *The Millennium Falcon*?

6) The religion Shinto comes from which country?

7) From which family of instruments is the tympani?

8) In the *Harry Potter* series of books, who was also known as Tom Riddle?

9) What English football team is known as the Gunners?

10) How is the Minnesota Mining and Manufacturing company better known?

Quiz 2
Round 5

1) Which company owned the liner known as The Titanic?

2) What is the capital city of Armenia?

3) In *The Simpsons*, name the principle of Springfield elementary school.

4) Who designed St. Paul's Cathedral in London?

5) The adjective 'pulmonary' refers to which organ?

6) Which automobile company makes the Mustang?

7) What country has the internet domain '.tv'?

8) What is the currency of The Vatican?

9) On what island does 'Thomas the Tank Engine' take place?

10) Where would you find George Best airport?

Quiz 2

Round 6

1) Which Winter Olympic sport involves sweeping, stones and brooms?

2) What was the name given to the period at the start of WWII, from September 1939 to May 1940, marked by a lack of military action?

3) Prior to the Euro, what was the currency of Cyprus?

4) In what year was the Declaration of American Independence signed?

5) Who wrote the book 'Little Women'?

6) Which U.S. state's capital is Columbus?

7) Which country is home to what was once called *The Millennium Dome*?

8) What Scot is credited with the invention of the television?

9) What European country is known in Latin as *Caledonia*?

10) What is the capital city of Greenland?

Quiz 2
Round 7

1) What is the capital city of Malta?

2) From what country do we get paella?

3) Who was the only British Prime Minister to be assassinated in Office?

4) On which Island group was Captain Cook killed in 1779?

5) In what country would you find Popocatepetl Mountain?

6) What tree is traditionally associated with the silk industry?

7) Who wrote the 'Discworld' books?

8) In ancient Rome, the emperor Caligula reportedly had an animal elected to the senate. What type of animal was it?

9) Who painted 'Girl with a pearl earring'?

10) Who wrote 'Hansel and Gretel'?

Quiz 2
Round 8

1) What is the name of Douglas Adams' paranoid android?

2) In western astrology, if you were born on the 1st of July, what sign would you be?

3) In what U.S city would you find O'Hare airport?

4) In olden days, what did a costermonger sell?

5) What Japanese word literally means empty orchestra?

6) Who did Sirhan Sirhan assassinate at the Ambassador Hotel in Los Angeles, June 1968?

7) What was the water-loving name of the lead singer with the group Marillion?

8) How was crusading King Richard I better known?

9) What is the state capital of Illinois, USA?

10) In which U.S. city is Eminem's *8-mile*?

Quiz 2
Round 9

1) In which desert would you find Death Valley?

2) Who was the leader of Egypt overthrown during the Arab Spring?

3) Who invented the diesel engine?

4) Which girl group was Beyoncé a part of before going solo?

5) What Latin term is used in English to describe something done for free?

6) Who was Britain's first female Prime-Minister?

7) Which famous British Physicist wrote *A Brief History of Time*?

8) What is the state capital of Florida, USA?

9) What was Indiana Jones' first name?

10) In Ten-pin Bowling, what is the name for 3 strikes in a row?

Quiz 2
Round 10

1) Who was the Russian Prime Minister on the 1st of January 2000?

2) Which actor from the show *Wizards of Waverly Place* performed the theme music?

3) Who famously walked out of Victor Verster Prison in 1990 after 27 years of incarceration?

4) Name the spacecraft which landed on the moon in 1969?

5) In television technology, what does LCD stand for?

6) What, in mental health, does OCD stand for?

7) What was the poet Philip Larkin's day job at Hull University?

8) What British player won the women's singles title at the 1968 U.S. Open?

9) Cos and romaine are types of what?

10) In Greek mythology, who is the king of the gods?

Quiz 3
Round 1

1) Who played James Bond in the movie *Skyfall*?

2) What type of music would you associate with the Grand Ole Opry?

3) What is the capital city of Saudi Arabia?

4) In which book did Magwitch escape from a prison ship?

5) Which golf venue set the standard of 18 holes per round?

6) From which country do we get the Hyundai brand?

7) From which metal does Argentina get its name?

8) Which country launched the first satellite into space?

9) What is the chemical symbol for Magnesium?

10) What is the currency of South Africa?

Quiz 3
Round 2

1) The Treaty of Paris, signed in 1782, ended which war?

2) What is the name given to a ring-shaped coral island, such as Bikini?

3) What rubber process was invented by Charles Goodyear?

4) In *The Pirates of the Caribbean* series of films, who played Will Turner?

5) What part of the body is affected by osteoporosis?

6) Who was the central historical character in the film *Braveheart*?

7) Who was the Roman messenger of the gods?

8) Fill in the blank in the NFL American Football team - The <blank> Vikings …

9) Where in the world would you be from if you were described as Monegasque?

10) After which Norse god do we get Wednesday?

Quiz 3

Round 3

1) How many hours in July?

2) Traditionally, a woman working as a logger was referred to as?

3) What cricketing minnow beat Pakistan in a shock result at the Cricket World Cup on the 17th of March 2007?

4) Which singer's birth name was Paul Hewson?

5) Who wrote 'A Clockwork Orange'?

6) Cartman, Kyle, Kenny and Stan are characters in which animated comedy TV show?

7) Fill in the blank in the NFL American Football team - The <blank> Cardinals …

8) One of the Seven Wonders of the Ancient World, who ordered built the Hanging Gardens of Babylon? His name is also used to describe a large bottle of champagne.

9) On a Qwerty keyboard, what letter begins the second row of letters?

10) TGV is the high-speed French train - what does the 'V' stand for?

Quiz 3

Round 4

1) In Bingo, what number is clickety-click?

2) What is the nickname of the Dutch professional darts player, Raymond Van Barneveld?

3) Which actor's birth name was Nicholas Coppola?

4) What are natives of Brittany called?

5) What is the capital city of Afghanistan?

6) Who composed Moonlight Sonata?

7) In what U.S city would you find JFK airport?

8) Which U.S. city is also known as 'The City of Brotherly Love'?

9) In what year was John Lennon assassinated?

10) If something is biannual, how often does it happen?

Quiz 3

Round 5

1) Hendrick Verwoerd is known as the architect of which system of racial segregation?

2) Pilot Manfred von Richthofen was better known by what nickname?

3) Which NBA team is based in Madison Square Garden?

4) Charolais and Limousin are breeds of what?

5) In what city would you find Dulles International airport?

6) Who painted 'Birth of Venus'?

7) What is the state capital of New York?

8) Who wrote 'The Odyssey' and 'The Iliad'?

9) In astrology which sign is represented by a water-bearer?

10) Who shot Lee Harvey Oswald?

Quiz 3

Round 6

1) In what war did the Siege of Ladysmith take place?

2) Who wrote 'Treasure Island'?

3) Who composed The Magic Flute?

4) How many players are on a polo team?

5) Where would you find John Lennon airport?

6) With what sport would you associate Annika Sörenstam?

7) In which English city would you find The Angel of the North?

8) What is the name for a camel with one hump?

9) What is the capital city of Libya?

10) Which American company had Jack Welsh as Chairman and CEO from 1981 and 2001?

Quiz 3

Round 7

1) According to Wikipedia, which genocidal English military and political leader died in 1658?

2) What was the destination of the Lusitania on her final voyage?

3) The singer Posh Spice named her first baby after which New York district?

4) Who was assassinated with an ice-pick in Mexico in 1940, by orders of Stalin.

5) What tuber is traditionally used to make poitín?

6) Christopher Cockerell floated into the record books with the invention of what?

7) Which school is missing from this list - Gryffindor, Slitheryn, Hufflepuff and ???

8) Which French car manufacturer made the 2CV and the DS?

9) In tennis, what does ATP stand for?

10) Which Soviet leader introduced the policy of *Glasnost*?

Quiz 3
Round 8

1) Who conquered Everest with Tenzing Norgay in 1953?

2) In darts, how many points does a bull's-eye score?

3) What car manufacturer made the Silver Ghost, Silver Shadow and Silver Cloud?

4) Traditionally, what gift should be given for a twenty-fifth wedding anniversary?

5) What was Dickens' last, unfinished book called?

6) Which US state is known as 'The Golden State'?

7) Who makes the *Les Paul* guitar?

8) Prior to the Euro, what was the currency of Portugal?

9) What is the national sport of Cuba?

10) Who composed *Carmina Burana*?

Quiz 3
Round 9

1) What name is given to the military nobility of medieval Japan?

2) Which desert is home to the Berber people?

3) What famous prehistoric monument was the subject of a song by Spinal Tap?

4) What chemical has the symbol C?

5) What is the first book of the Bible?

6) What is the largest organ of the human body?

7) What is the last letter of the Greek alphabet?

8) Jack Bauer appeared in what time-sensitive TV series?

9) Who had a hit with "White Christmas" in 1942?

10) In Egyptian mythology, who was the evil god of storms and disorder?

Quiz 3
Round 10

1) What is the capital city of Nicaragua?
2) In the film 'Dodgeball' , what is the governing body of dodgeball called?
3) What is a scimitar?
4) How many hours in a week?
5) Which Native American tribe was massacred at Wounded Knee?
6) In the litmus test, what colour is an acid?
7) Which Hungarian is credited with the invention of the ballpoint pen?
8) Who was the first unseeded tennis player to win Wimbledon?
9) In the *Lord of the Rings* films, who plays Gollum?
10) With what religion would you associate The Torah?

Quiz 4
Round 1

1) What is the capital city of Argentina?

2) What is the state capital of Minnesota?

3) What is Thomas Edison's middle name?

4) In what country would you find Knock airport?

5) What plant leaf features on the rugby jerseys of the All Blacks?

6) What fruit is used to make Calvados?

7) What is the state capital of Alabama?

8) What country has the internet domain '.cn'?

9) What does the 'B' in car manufacturer BMW stand for?

10) Who wrote 'The Ballad of Reading Gaol'?

Quiz 4
Round 2

1) Which poem famously begins - 'I wandered lonely as a cloud'?

2) Prior to the Euro, what was the currency of Ireland?

3) Who shot John Lennon?

4) In Harry Potter, which family lives at No.4 Privet Drive?

5) In astrology which sign is represented by a scales?

6) What name is shared by a heavy metal band and a torture device which uses spikes inside a cabinet to impale victims?

7) Who was the lead singer of *Duran Duran*?

8) Who composed *The William Tell Overture*?

9) Which disease is also known as German Measles?

10) Which big screen adaption of a Roald Dahl book featured Jeremy Irons and his son Samuel playing the lead roles?

Quiz 4
Round 3

1) Who did James Earl Ray shoot in Memphis in 1968?

2) Where in your body would you find your tarsels?

3) What does R.E.M. stand for?

4) Who wrote 'The Jungle Book'?

5) How many faces does a dodecahedron have?

6) If something is biennial, how often does it occur?

7) What European country is known in Latin as *Hibernia*?

8) Who, according to the Bible, saw his wife turn to a pillar of salt?

9) Who invented bi-focal glasses?

10) What is the chemical symbol for Nickel?

Quiz 4
Round 4

1) What country hosted the inaugural FIFA World Cup in 1930?

2) Winston Smith smoked Victory cigarettes in which book?

3) Which singer's birth name was Katheryn Elizabeth Hudson?

4) Traditionally, what gift should be given for a fiftieth wedding anniversary?

5) In the hit U.S. comedy *Malcolm in the Middle*, who played Malcolm?

6) In what year did World War II start?

7) What is the capital city of Vietnam?

8) In what town does Spongebob live?

9) Which Norwegian politician's actions in Worlds War II led to his surname being a byword for collaboration?

10) Who painted 'Vase with 15 Sunflowers'?

Quiz 4

Round 5

1) What is the chemical symbol for Mercury?

2) What is the state capital of Arizona, USA?

3) What is the name of the small pieces of wood that sit atop the stumps in cricket?

4) In which UK city would you find The Gorbals?

5) What is the capital city of Uruguay?

6) Which famous revolutionary was shot dead in La Higuera, Vallegrande, Bolivia, in October 1967?

7) Who wrote the short story on which The Shawshank Redemption is based?

8) Robespierre is associated with which revolution?

9) Who is the main character in William Boyd's *Solo*?

10) Which U.S. State was the last to join the Union?

Quiz 4

Round 6

1) Which is the most populous U.S. city?

2) Northern Rhodesian is now known as?

3) Operation Barbarossa was the name for the German invasion of what country in WWII?

4) Which word, used to describe a tidal wave, has been taken into English from Japanese?

5) What do Argentinians call The Falkland Islands?

6) Who wrote 'Peter Pan'?

7) What is the name of the Israeli parliament?

8) What was the subtitle of the first *Lord of the Rings* movie?

9) What Latin term is used in English to mean *seize the day*?

10) In what year was the Battle of Waterloo?

Quiz 4

Round 7

1)   What kind of an animal was the children's character Curious George?

2)   Who created the detective 'Hercule Poirot'?

3)   'Between my finger and my thumb
     The squat pen rests. I'll dig with it.' - Name the Nobel Laureate.

4)   A wind instrument developed by Indigenous Australians of northern Australia, it is sometimes described as a natural wooden trumpet or drone pipe - what is it?

5)   What country do the French call *Le Pays Des Galles*?

6)   What was the name of the boat that Darwin sailed to Galapagos?

7)   What is the name of the mystery-solving cartoon dog whose best friend is called Shaggy?

8)   With which religion do we associate the great Sultan Saladin?

9)   Who wrote the story that 'Walter Mitty' is based on?

10) Prior to the Euro, what was the currency of Greece?

Quiz 4
Round 8

1) Which festival literally translates as *Fat Tuesday*?
2) What is James Bond's family motto?
3) 'He wishes for the cloths of heaven' was written by which poet?
4) Sunni and Shia are denominations of which religion?
5) Where was Paddington Bear born?
6) What is the capital city of Turkey?
7) "Once upon a time there were three little girls who went to the police academy..." is the opening line from which TV show's Theme song?
8) Who wrote the political philosophy entitled *The Prince*?
9) Which monarch was the intended victim of the Gunpowder Plot of 1605?
10) What is the capital city of Philippines?

Quiz 4

Round 9

1) What is the capital city of Iraq?

2) What was the name of Ricky Gervais' character in *The Office*?

3) Which character regularly died in most episodes in the early seasons of South Park?

4) What is the last book of the Bible?

5) Which Italian explorer finally returned home in 1295, having wandered Asia with his father and his uncle for 24 years?

6) Which is chronologically the first of the four Grand Slam tennis tournaments, taking place in the last fortnight of January?

7) For what international cricket team did Don Bradman play?

8) Which President of the US was indicted during the Watergate scandal?

9) 'The Rime of the Ancient Mariner' - Name the poet who wrote this masterpiece.

10) In Star Wars, what was C3PO?

Quiz 4
Round 10

1) Which team has won the most number of NBA finals?

2) Who captained the English cricket team that infamously toured Australia in 1932/33 in what was called The Bodyline Series?

3) In maths, what letter is used to represent the square root of -1?

4) In Television technology, what does LED stand for?

5) *Krav Maga* is a self-defence technique associated with which country?

6) What is the longest river in Italy?

7) What is the name of the oven used to fire pottery?

8) Normally, what flavour are the drinks Pastis, Sambuca and Ouzo?

9) In cricket, what is the term for a lower-order batsman who comes in to bat higher up the order than usual near the end of the day's play?

10) Which Irish-born actor succeeded Richard Harris in the role of Dumbledore?

Quiz 5
Round 1

1) In soccer, what does the first 'F' in FIFA stand for?

2) Which country, founded by The American Colonisation Society in 1821, declared independence in 1847?

3) What is the formal name for the collar bone, in the human skeleton?

4) What is the capital city of Bosnia and Herzegovina?

5) Which U.S. state's capital is Salem?

6) Which country's flag is Ireland's flag in reverse?

7) What is the name of the French game, played over gravel, where a large ball is thrown so as to land as close as possible to a smaller ball?

8) The NBA Basketball team - the <blank> Jazz. Fill in the blank…

9) In what year was the Magna Carta signed?

10) What is the state capital of Arkansas, USA?

Quiz 5
Round 2

1) What does the 'E' in UNICEF stand for?

2) This city was once known as Petrograd and then Leningrad but what is it called now?

3) Which writer's birth name was Eric Arthur Blair?

4) One of the Seven Wonders of the Ancient World, what was the name of the giant statue that bestrode the harbour at Rhodes?

5) In what year was the Battle of Hastings?

6) What colour do you get if you mix red and yellow?

7) Which mountain range is known as *The Backbone of Italy*?

8) While Armstrong and Aldrin walked on the moon, who stayed behind in the capsule?

9) Who painted 'The Scream'?

10) Which monarch ruled Britain from 1837 to 1901?

Quiz 5

Round 3

1) In the atom, what are the neutral particles called?

2) In the internet, what does URL stand for?

3) Chester Carlson invented which piece of office equipment?

4) Who was the captain of The Bounty before the mutiny?

5) In the U.S. version of The Office, who played Michael Scott, Regional Manager of Dunder Mifflin?

6) Who discovered penicillin?

7) What drink is normally poured over Crèpe Suzette and ignited?

8) In Roman Numerals, what does MM mean?

9) Which Mediterranean island was home to the Minoan civilisation?

10) In the *Lord of the Rings* films, who plays Gandalf?

Quiz 5

Round 4

1) How is acetylsalicylic acid better known?

2) Who was the U.S. President at the outbreak of WWII?

3) Which British-Jamaican Rastafarian writer and poet's middle names are 'Obadiah Iqbal'?

4) In literature, who is the housekeeper at 221b Baker Street?

5) What is the capital city of North Korea?

6) What is the name of Spongebob's starfish friend?

7) How many cents in a nickel?

8) In Lawn Bowls, what is the name of the small target ball?

9) What is the common name for the *Aurora Borealis*?

10) Which MLB baseball team is based in Wrigley Field?

Quiz 5

Round 5

1) In Roman Numerals, what does D mean?

2) If something is described as ovine, then what is it like?

3) Which is the only Great Lake entirely within the U.S.?

4) From which flower do we get saffron?

5) Who painted 'Ceci n'est pas une pipe'?

6) In medicine, how do we normally refer to the tubercle bacillus?

7) What fruit are Valencia, Jaffa and Joppa types of?

8) What year did the Korean War end?

9) Who was U.S. President on the 1st of January 2000?

10) What is the chemical symbol for Sulphur?

Quiz 5

Round 6

1) Which star of the hit comedy *How I met Your Mother* first came to our attention as Doogie Howser M.D.?

2) What is the capital city of Haiti?

3) In which European city would you find The Little Mermaid?

4) What country has the internet domain '.va'?

5) What is the capital city of Syria?

6) What was the name of the semi-autonomous, Nazi puppet government of France in WWII?

7) What is the area of Africa once known as Nyasaland now known as?

8) What are the only team outside of the U.S. to have won a MLB World Series?

9) Prior to the Euro, what was the currency of Belgium?

10) Which Emperor died on Saint Helena in 1821?

Quiz 5
Round 7

1) Which Afrikaans word, literally meaning 'separateness' is used to describe a policy of racial segregation?

2) Lincoln, Washington, Roosevelt - which President is missing from the Mount Rushmore four?

3) Which country gifted The Statue of Liberty to the USA?

4) Which mythical twins, raised by a wolf, supposedly founded ancient Rome?

5) Which inventor was known as The Wizard of Menlo Park?

6) In Hamlet, fill in the blank: "There are more things in heaven and earth, <blank>, than are dreamt of in your philosophy…

7) If a dish is described as florentine, what vegetable must it contain?

8) Which musician's birth name was Richard Starkey?

9) In darts, what is the largest score that can be achieved with one dart?

10) Who succeeded Julius Caesar as Roman Emperor?

Quiz 5

Round 8

1) NaCl, Sodium Chloride, is better known as what?

2) In astrology which sign is represented by a ram?

3) What chemical has the symbol Fe?

4) What is Carnophobia a fear of?

5) In astrology which sign is represented by a goat?

6) In the TV series House, what was Dr. House's first name?

7) Sveyn Forkbeard ruled which European country from 1013-1014, having usurped Ethelred the Unready?

8) Of what University is Trinity College Dublin the sole college?

9) Prior to the Euro, what was the currency of Monaco?

10) In the TV series Homeland, who played CIA agent Carrie Mathison?

Quiz 5
Round 9

1) In Roman Numerals, what does M mean?

2) Who composed *Rhapsody in Blue*?

3) What is the capital city of Austria?

4) Which Dickens book features a character called Pip?

5) When the Channel Tunnel was opened, the ceremony was overseen by President Mitterrand for France and but who represented England?

6) What is the longest river in France?

7) In Greek and Roman Mythology, what was the name of the 3-headed hellhound?

8) In what year was the Great Fire of London?

9) From what country do we get a dish called *tartiflette*?

10) What is the square-root of 144?

Quiz 5
Round 10

1) What is the state capital of Colorado, USA?

2) In Japan, what is *wasabi*?

3) Who was U.K. Prime Minister on the 1st of January 2000?

4) Who won Best Actor in the 2012 Oscars for *Lincoln*?

5) What is the capital city of Colombia?

6) In which book might you spend a *malenky bit of cutter*?

7) Thompson Seedless and Zante Black Corinth are types of what?

8) A Russian folk stringed musical instrument with a characteristic triangular body and three strings - what is it?

9) Who was the Bond villain in *Moonraker*?

10) What is the capital city of Egypt?

Tiebreakers

1) Who is the Roman god of the sea?

2) Which country is also known as 'The Land of the Rising Sun'?

3) What sort of sea-creature is a Portugese Man-of-War?

4) Who wrote 'Death in Venice'?

5) What is Southern Rhodesia now known as?

6) What country has the internet domain '.au'?

7) According to Greek legend, what creature dwelt at the centre of the Cretan Labyrinth?

8) Who wrote 'Portrait of Dorian Grey'?

9) In chemistry, organic compounds always contain which element?

10) In the comedy series *The Big Bang Theory*, what is Howard's surname?

11) In Television technology, what does CRT stand for?

12) Who invented dynamite?

13) The Humerus, Ulna and what are the three bones in the human arm?

14) Guy Pierce played a teacher in which Australian soap opera?

15) Which U.S. state is nicknamed 'The Garden State'?

16) Which English soap takes place in Weatherfield?

17) What is the capital city of Cuba?

18) Which saint's day falls on the 6th of December?

19) Which actor's birth name was Maurice Micklewhite?

20) In The Simpsons, what instrument does Lisa play?

The Answers

Quiz 1

Round 1

1) Who wrote 'Chitty Chitty Bang Bang'?
Ian Fleming
2) Who wrote the Artemis Fowl series?
Eoin Colfer
3) Who invented basketball?
Dr. James Naismith
4) In astrology which sign is represented by a bull?
Taurus
5) What is the longest river in Ireland?
Shannon
6) Which German car manufacturer is associated with the 911, Cayenne and Boxter?
Porsche
7) Which Dickens book features Dothebys Hall?
Nicholas Nickleby
8) What is the name given to a violent riot started to massacre an ethnic or religious group?
Pogrom
9) Who created the comic *Tin Tin*?
Herg?/Georges Remi
10) How many bytes in 1 kilobyte, in computer terminology?
1024

Quiz 1

Round 2

1) What is the capital city of Hungary?
   Budapest
2) How many pockets does a Snooker table have?
   6
3) According to Norse legend, after dying in battle a soldier goes to which hall?
   Valhalla
4) In what year did World War One end?
   1918
5) Which T.S. Eliot poem features the famous 'not with a bang' line?
   The Hollow Men
6) Who was the last Tsar of Russia?
   Nicholas II
7) Who composed *The Hallelujah Chorus*?
   Handel
8) In Major League Baseball, if the first New York team is the Yankees, what is the second?
   Mets
9) Kale, cabbage and broccoli are part of which plant genus?
   Brassica
10) Which rapper's birth name was Curtis Jackson?
    50 Cent

Quiz 1
Round 3

1) Yehudi Menuhin was famously associated with which instrument?
Violin

2) In which country would you find the Cliffs of Moher?
Ireland

3) Which word, used to describe feeling joy at someone's misery, has been taken into English from German?
Schadenfreude

4) What is the name of the fasting month in Islam?
Ramadan

5) Which member of *The Fast Show* cast wrote the Young James Bond series of books?
Charlie Higson

6) In the animated film *Kung Fu Panda*, who voiced Master Shifu?
Dustin Hoffman

7) Who directed *Jurassic Park*(1993)?
Stephen Spielberg

8) Dying in BC 71, what was the name of the slave leader who led a revolt against the Romans and would be portrayed by Kirk Douglas in film?
Spartacus

9) Which book's eponymous heroine fell in love with Mr. Rochester?
Jane Eyre

10) What country has the internet domain '.ca'?
Canada

Quiz 1

Round 4

1) In the UK, what was added to the town names of Beeston, Bognor and Lyme
   Regis

2) In golf, what is also known as a three strokes under par or a 'double eagle'?
   Albatross

3) What is the name given in India to elephant drivers?
   Mahouts

4) In which U.S. city would you find the *Country Music Hall of Fame*?
   Nashville

5) Australia made a significant change to the $5 note in 2000 - what did they remove?
   The Queen

6) Fill in the blank in the NFL American Football team - The <blank> Eagles ...
   Philadelphia

7) Who wrote the book 'I know why the caged bird sings'?
   Maya Anjelou

8) What is the smallest organ of the human body?
   Pineal Gland

9) Which classic British comedy features Del Boy and Rodney?
   Only Fools and Horses

10) Who was the lead singer of *The Boomtown Rats*?
    Bob Geldof

Quiz 1

Round 5

1) Who painted 'The Mona Lisa'?
   Leonardo Da Vinci
2) Which country's flag features a cedar?
   Lebanon
3) Which volcano erupted in AD79, destroying the town of Herculaneum?
   Mount Vesuvius
4) Who wrote the book 'Northern Lights'?
   Phillip Pullman
5) What country's capital city is Bratislava?
   Slovakia
6) Which island group's name comes from the Latin for the *Island of the Dogs*?
   Canaries
7) In which year was the first modern Olympics held?
   1896
8) With which religion would you associate The Koran?   Islam
9) On a Qwerty keyboard, what is the last letter on the second row of letters?
   L
10) Who directed *Blade Runner* (1982)?
    Ridley Scott

Quiz 1

Round 6

1) How old was Harry Potter when he entered Hogwarts?
11

2) In metres, how long is an Olympic swimming pool?
50 Metres

3) What cartoon family lives at *39 Stone Canyon Way*?
The Flintstones

4) Which English football team plays at Anfield?
Liverpool

5) Who is the Greek goddess of love?
Aphrodite

6) Which singer's birth name was Robert Zimmerman?
Bob Dylan

7) In bingo, what number is two fat ladies?
88

8) In astrology which sign is represented by a fish?
Pisces

9) In 2000 who released the album *The Marshall Mathers LP*?
Eminem

10) What fruit is traditionally used to make Kirsch?
Cherries

Quiz 1

Round 7

1) Which MLB baseball team is based in Fenway Park?
Boston Red Sox
2) In what mountain range is Mont Blanc?
Alps
3) Which Jewish holy day is also known as *The Day of Atonement*?
Yom Kippur
4) What was the surname of Truman, in the movie *The Truman Show*?
Burbank
5) *Richard of York Gave Battle in Vain* is a mnemonic for what?
Colours of the rainbow
6) What is Claustrophobia a fear of?
Confined Spaces
7) Which classic comedy features three priests on Craggy Island?
Father Ted
8) How many points is a yellow ball worth in snooker?
2
9) In the 1960 film Psycho, what was the name of the motel?
Bates Motel
10) Which famous general was killed at The Battle of the Little Bighorn?
General Custer

Quiz 1

Round 8

1) Who was the first man in space?
Yuri Gagarin

2) In emails, what does BCC stand for?
Blind carbon copy

3) Who composed *The Ride of the Valkyries*?
Wagner

4) Who was the Russian Leader at the outbreak of WWII?
Stalin

5) Which cartoon family lives at 744 Evergreen Terrace?
The Flanders

6) Which important political position has been held by Kurt Waldheim and Boutros Boutros Ghali?
U.N General Secretary

7) Fill in the blank in the NFL American Football team - The Cleveland <blank> …
Browns

8) From what American Indian tribe was Geronimo?
Apache

9) Which automobile company makes the Prius?
Toyota

10) Poland and Belgium share what national flower?
Red Poppy

Quiz 1
Round 9

1) How is a Chinese gooseberry better known?
   Kiwi-Fruit
2) Which conference to decide the post-war division of Europe took place after the Tehran Conference and before the Potsdam conference?
   The Yalta Conference
3) Which writer's birth name was Samuel Longhorne Clemens?
   Mark Twain
4) What is the capital city of Liechtenstein?
   Vaduz
5) What fruit are Concord, Conference and Beth types of?
   Pear
6) What was the Allied code-name for the Battle of Normandy?
   Operation Overlord
7) What famous drink is associated with St. James' Gate in Dublin, Ireland?
   Guinness
8) Which famous playwright married Marilyn Monroe?
   Arthur Miller
9) Which playwright became the first president of the Czech Republic in 1993?
   Václav Havel
10) Which military organisation's motto is 'Legio Patria Nostra'?
    The French Foreign Legion

Quiz 1

Round 10

1) Which Shakespeare play features Polonius?
   Hamlet
2) From which type of flower do we get vanilla?
   Orchid
3) What do the letters *USB* stand for in electronics?
   Universal Serial Bus
4) Which is the largest South American country?
   Brazil
5) What is the capital city of South Korea?
   Seoul
6) Who won the Best Actress Oscar in 2011 for *The Iron Lady*?
   Meryl Streep
7) Who wrote 'Portrait of the Artist as a Young Man'?
   James Joyce
8) How is Jorge Mario Bergoglio better known?
   Pope Francis
9) With which sport would you associate the nicknames Whirlwind and Hurricane?
   Snooker
10) Who was the U.K. Prime Minister at the outbreak of WWII?
    Neville Chamberlain

Quiz 2

Round 1

1) What is the capital city of Singapore?
Singapore
2) Which European country gave women the vote in 1986?
Liechtenstein
3) Which toy was invented by Ole Kirk Christiansen?
Lego
4) In which city were the first modern Olympics held?
Athens
5) Which desert's name is based on the Tswana word for 'great thirst'?
Kalahari
6) In photography, what does SLR mean?
Single Lens Reflex
7) In Norse mythology, who was the allfather of the Gods and ruler of Asgard?
Odin
8) What is the capital city of Croatia?
Zagreb
9) Who founded The Church of Scientology?
L. Ron Hubbard
10) What are Braeburn, Golden Delicious and Pink Lady types of?
Apple

Quiz 2

Round 2

1) Who was granted the first telephone patent?
   Alexander Graham Bell
2) Who played Tonto in the 2013 film *The Lone Ranger*?
   Johnny Depp
3) What chemical has the symbol He?
   Helium
4) Which letter of the alphabet has more than one syllable?
   W
5) Amarillo, on Route 66, gets its name from the Spanish for what colour?
   Yellow
6) In the atom, what are the positively charged particles called?
   Protons
7) What is the state capital of Alaska?
   Juneau
8) In what city would you find Schiphol airport?
   Amsterdam
9) Who was the first man to walk on the moon?
   Neil Armstrong
10) What is the capital city of New Zealand?
   Wellington

Quiz 2

Round 3

1) What name was given to the Spanish and Portuguese explorer-soldiers from the fifteenth to seventeenth centuries?
   Conquistadors

2) In 2012, who won a Record of the Year Grammy with 'Rolling in the Deep'?
   Adele

3) What name is derived from the Greek for 'terrible lizard'?
   Dinosaur

4) What in computers is RAM?
   Random Access Memory

5) Which comedy duo starred in the British comedy series from 1990 to 1993 as Jeeves and Wooster?
   Stephen Fry and Hugh Laurie

6) In the U.S. it is called Saran Wrap - what is it called in the U.K.?
   Cling-film

7) What is the first letter of the Greek alphabet?
   Alpha

8) In database programming, what does SQL stand for?
   Structured Query Language

9) Fill in the blank in the NFL American Football team - The Green Bay <blank> …
   Packers

10) 'Do not go gentle into that good night' was written by which poet?
    Dylan Thomas

Quiz 2

Round 4

1) Which word, used to describe an extensive array of food, has been taken into English from Swedish?
Smorgasbord

2) In what country was poet Pablo Neruda born?
Chile

3) What country do the French call Angleterre?
England

4) Which Shakespeare play features the Moor of Venice?
Othello

5) In Star Wars, what was *The Millennium Falcon*?
Spacecraft

6) The religion Shinto comes from which country?
Japan

7) From which family of instruments is the tympani?
Percussion

8) In the *Harry Potter* series of books, who was also known as Tom Riddle?
Lord Voldemort

9) What English football team is known as the Gunners?
Arsenal

10) How is the Minnesota Mining and Manufacturing company better known?
3M

Quiz 2

Round 5

1) Which company owned the liner known as The Titanic?
White Star Line

2) What is the capital city of Armenia?
Yerevan

3) In The Simpsons, name the principle of Springfield elementary school.
Principle Seymour Skinner

4) Who designed St. Paul's Cathedral in London?
Sir Christopher Wren

5) The adjective 'pulmonary' refers to which organ?
Lungs

6) Which automobile company makes the Mustang?
Ford

7) What country has the internet domain '.tv'?
Tuvalu

8) What is the currency of The Vatican?
Euro

9) On what island does 'Thomas the Tank Engine' take place?
Sodor

10) Where would you find George Best airport?
Belfast

Quiz 2

Round 6

1) Which Winter Olympic sport involves sweeping, stones and brooms?
Curling

2) What was the name given to the period at the start of WWII, from September 1939 to May 1940, marked by a lack of military action?
The Phoney War

3) Prior to the Euro, what was the currency of Cyprus?
Pound

4) In what year was the Declaration of American Independence signed?
1776

5) Who wrote the book 'Little Women'?
Louise May Alcott

6) Which U.S. state's capital is Columbus?
Ohio

7) Which country is home to what was once called *The Millennium Dome*?
England

8) What Scot is credited with the invention of the television?
John Logie Baird

9) What European country is known in Latin as *Caledonia*?
Scotland

10) What is the capital city of Greenland?
Nuuk

Quiz 2

Round 7

1) What is the capital city of Malta?
Valletta

2) From what country do we get paella?
Spain

3) Who was the only British Prime Minister to be assassinated in Office?
Spencer Percival

4) On which Island group was Captain Cook killed in 1779?
Hawaii/Sandwich isles

5) In what country would you find Popocatepetl Mountain?
Mexico

6) What tree is traditionally associated with the silk industry?
Mulberry

7) Who wrote the 'Discworld' books?
Terry Pratchett

8) In ancient Rome, the emperor Caligula reportedly had an animal elected to the senate. What type of animal was it?
Horse

9) Who painted 'Girl with a pearl earring'?
Jan Vermeer

10) Who wrote 'Hansel and Gretel'?
The Brothers Grimm

Quiz 2

Round 8

1) What is the name of Douglas Adams' paranoid android?
Marvin

2) In western astrology, if you were born on the 1st of July, what sign would you be?
Cancer

3) In what U.S city would you find O'Hare airport?
Chicago

4) In olden days, what did a costermonger sell?
Fruit and veg

5) What Japanese word literally means empty orchestra?
Karaoke

6) Who did Sirhan Sirhan assassinate at the Ambassador Hotel in Los Angeles, June 1968?
Bobby Kennedy

7) What was the water-loving name of the lead singer with the group Marillion?
Fish

8) How was crusading King Richard I better known?
Richard The Lionheart

9) What is the state capital of Illinois, USA?
Springfield

10) In which U.S. city is Eminem's *8-mile*?
Detroit

Quiz 2

Round 9

1) In which desert would you find Death Valley?
   Mojave
2) Who was the leader of Egypt overthrown during the Arab Spring?
   Hosni Mubarak
3) Who invented the diesel engine?
   Rudolph Diesel
4) Which girl group was Beyoncé a part of before going solo?
   Destiny's Child
5) What Latin term is used in English to describe something done for free?
   Pro bono
6) Who was Britain's first female Prime-Minister?
   Margaret Thatcher
7) Which famous British Physicist wrote *A Brief History of Time*?
   Stephen Hawking
8) What is the state capital of Florida, USA?
   Tallahassee
9) What was Indiana Jones' first name?
   Henry
10) In Ten-pin Bowling, what is the name for 3 strikes in a row?
    A Turkey

Quiz 2

Round 10

1) Who was the Russian Prime Minister on the 1st of January 2000?
Vladimir Putin

2) Which actor from the show *Wizards of Waverly Place* performed the theme music?
Selena Gomez

3) Who famously walked out of Victor Verster Prison in 1990 after 27 years of incarceration?
Nelson Mandela

4) Name the spacecraft which landed on the moon in 1969?
Apollo 11

5) In television technology, what does LCD stand for?
Liquid Crystal Display

6) What, in mental health, does OCD stand for?
Obsessive Compulsive Disorder

7) What was the poet Philip Larkin's day job at Hull University?
Librarian

8) What British player won the women's singles title at the 1968 U.S. Open?
Virginia Wade

9) Cos and romaine are types of what?
Lettuce

10) In Greek mythology, who is the king of the gods?
Zeus

Quiz 3
Round 1

1) Who played James Bond in the movie *Skyfall*?
   Daniel Craig
2) What type of music would you associate with the Grand Ole Opry?
   Country Music
3) What is the capital city of Saudi Arabia?
   Riyadh
4) In which book did Magwitch escape from a prison ship?
   Great Expectations
5) Which golf venue set the standard of 18 holes per round?
   St. Andrews, Scotland
6) From which country do we get the Hyundai brand?
   South Korea
7) From which metal does Argentina get its name?
   Silver
8) Which country launched the first satellite into space?
   USSR
9) What is the chemical symbol for Magnesium?
   Mg
10) What is the currency of South Africa?
   Rand

Quiz 3

Round 2

1) The Treaty of Paris, signed in 1782, ended which war?
American War of Independence

2) What is the name given to a ring-shaped coral island, such as Bikini?
Atoll

3) What rubber process was invented by Charles Goodyear?
Vulcanisation

4) In *The Pirates of the Caribbean* series of films, who played Will Turner?
Orlando Bloom

5) What part of the body is affected by osteoporosis?
Bones

6) Who was the central historical character in the film *Braveheart*?
William Wallace

7) Who was the Roman messenger of the gods?
Mercury

8) Fill in the blank in the NFL American Football team - The <blank> Vikings …
Minnesota

9) Where in the world would you be from if you were described as Monegasque?
Monaco

10) After which Norse god do we get Wednesday?
Woden/Odin

Quiz 3

Round 3

1) How many hours in July?
5208

2) Traditionally, a woman working as a logger was referred to as?
A Lumberjill

3) What cricketing minnow beat Pakistan in a shock result at the Cricket World Cup on the 17th of March 2007?
Ireland

4) Which singer's birth name was Paul Hewson?
Bono (Vox)

5) Who wrote 'A Clockwork Orange'?
Anthony Burgess

6) Cartman, Kyle, Kenny and Stan are characters in which animated comedy TV show?
South Park

7) Fill in the blank in the NFL American Football team - The <blank> Cardinals …
Arizona

8) One of the Seven Wonders of the Ancient World, who ordered built the Hanging Gardens of Babylon? His name is also used to describe a large bottle of champagne.
Nebuchadnezzar II

9) On a Qwerty keyboard, what letter begins the second row of letters?
A

10) TGV is the high-speed French train - what does the 'V' stand for?
Vitesse

Quiz 3

Round 4

1) In Bingo, what number is clickety-click?
66

2) What is the nickname of the Dutch professional darts player, Raymond Van Barneveld?
Barney

3) Which actor's birth name was Nicholas Coppola?
Nicolas Cage

4) What are natives of Brittany called?
Bretons

5) What is the capital city of Afghanistan?
Kabul

6) Who composed Moonlight Sonata?
Beethoven

7) In what U.S city would you find JFK airport?
New York

8) Which U.S. city is also known as 'The City of Brotherly Love'?
Philadelphia

9) In what year was John Lennon assassinated?
1980

10) If something is biannual, how often does it happen?
Twice a year

Quiz 3

Round 5

1) Hendrick Verwoerd is known as the architect of which system of racial segregation?
Apartheid

2) Pilot Manfred von Richthofen was better known by what nickname?
The Red Baron

3) Which NBA team is based in Madison Square Garden?
NY Nicks

4) Charolais and Limousin are breeds of what?
Cows

5) In what city would you find Dulles International airport?
Washington D.C.

6) Who painted 'Birth of Venus'?
Sandro Botticelli

7) What is the state capital of New York?
Albany

8) Who wrote 'The Odyssey' and 'The Iliad'?
Homer

9) In astrology which sign is represented by a water-bearer?
Aquarius

10) Who shot Lee Harvey Oswald?
Jack Ruby

Quiz 3

Round 6

1) In what war did the Siege of Ladysmith take place?
The Boer War
2) Who wrote 'Treasure Island'?
Robert Louis Stephenson
3) Who composed The Magic Flute?
Mozart
4) How many players are on a polo team?
4
5) Where would you find John Lennon airport?
Liverpool
6) With what sport would you associate Annika Sörenstam?
Golf
7) In which English city would you find The Angel of the North?
Gateshead
8) What is the name for a camel with one hump?
Dromedary
9) What is the capital city of Libya?
Tripoli
10) Which American company had Jack Welsh as Chairman and CEO from 1981 and 2001?
General Electric

Quiz 3

Round 7

1) According to Wikipedia, which genocidal English military and political leader died in 1658?
Oliver Cromwell

2) What was the destination of the Lusitania on her final voyage?
Liverpool

3) The singer Posh Spice named her first baby after which New York district?
Brooklyn

4) Who was assassinated with an ice-pick in Mexico in 1940, by orders of Stalin.
Leon Trotsky

5) What tuber is traditionally used to make poitín?
Potato

6) Christopher Cockerell floated into the record books with the invention of what?
Hovercraft

7) Which school is missing from this list - Gryffindor, Slitheryn, Hufflepuff and ???
Ravenclaw

8) Which French car manufacturer made the 2CV and the DS?
Citroën

9) In tennis, what does ATP stand for?
Association of Tennis Professionals

10) Which Soviet leader introduced the policy of *Glasnost*?
Mikhail Gorbachev

Quiz 3

Round 8

1) Who conquered Everest with Tenzing Norgay in 1953?
Edmund Hillary

2) In darts, how many points does a bull's-eye score?
50

3) What car manufacturer made the Silver Ghost, Silver Shadow and Silver Cloud?
Rolls-Royce

4) Traditionally, what gift should be given for a twenty-fifth wedding anniversary?
Silver

5) What was Dickens' last, unfinished book called?
The Mystery of Edwin Drood

6) Which US state is known as 'The Golden State'?
California

7) Who makes the *Les Paul* guitar?
Gibson

8) Prior to the Euro, what was the currency of Portugal?
Escudo

9) What is the national sport of Cuba?
Baseball

10) Who composed *Carmina Burana*?
Carl Orff

Quiz 3

Round 9

1) What name is given to the military nobility of medieval Japan?
Samurai

2) Which desert is home to the Berber people?
Sahara

3) What famous prehistoric monument was the subject of a song by Spinal Tap?
Stonehenge

4) What chemical has the symbol C?
Carbon

5) What is the first book of the Bible?
Genesis

6) What is the largest organ of the human body?
Skin

7) What is the last letter of the Greek alphabet?
Omega

8) Jack Bauer appeared in what time-sensitive TV series?
24

9) Who had a hit with "White Christmas" in 1942?
Bing Crosby

10) In Egyptian mythology, who was the evil god of storms and disorder?
Set or Seth

Quiz 3

Round 10

1) What is the capital city of Nicaragua?
Managua
2) In the film 'Dodgeball' , what is the governing body of dodgeball called?
The American Dodgeball Association of America
3) What is a scimitar?
A curved sword
4) How many hours in a week?
168
5) Which Native American tribe was massacred at Wounded Knee?
Lakota
6) In the litmus test, what colour is an acid?
Pink/Red
7) Which Hungarian is credited with the invention of the ballpoint pen?
Lazlo Biro
8) Who was the first unseeded tennis player to win Wimbledon?
Borris Becker
9) In the *Lord of the Rings* films, who plays Gollum?
Andy Serkis
10) With what religion would you associate The Torah?
Judaism

Quiz 4

Round 1

1) What is the capital city of Argentina?
Buenos Aires

2) What is the state capital of Minnesota?
Saint Paul

3) What is Thomas Edison's middle name?
Alva

4) In what country would you find Knock airport?
Ireland

5) What plant leaf features on the rugby jerseys of the All Blacks?
Silver Fern

6) What fruit is used to make Calvados?
Apples

7) What is the state capital of Alabama?
Montgomery

8) What country has the internet domain '.cn'?
China

9) What does the 'B' in car manufacturer BMW stand for?
Bavarian/Bayerische

10) Who wrote 'The Ballad of Reading Gaol'?
Oscar Wilde

Quiz 4

Round 2

1) Which poem famously begins - 'I wandered lonely as a cloud'?
Daffodils

2) Prior to the Euro, what was the currency of Ireland?
Punt/Irish Pound

3) Who shot John Lennon?
Mark Chapman

4) In Harry Potter, which family lives at No.4 Privet Drive?
The Dursleys

5) In astrology which sign is represented by a scales?
Libra

6) What name is shared by a heavy metal band and a torture device which uses spikes inside a cabinet to impale victims?
Iron Maiden

7) Who was the lead singer of *Duran Duran*?
Simon LeBon

8) Who composed *The William Tell Overture*?
Rossini

9) Which disease is also known as German Measles?
Rubella

10) Which big screen adaption of a Roald Dahl book featured Jeremy Irons and his son Samuel playing the lead roles?
Danny, The Champion of the World

Quiz 4

Round 3

1) Who did James Earl Ray shoot in Memphis in 1968?
   Martin Luther King Jnr
2) Where in your body would you find your tarsels?
   Foot
3) What does R.E.M. stand for?
   Rapid Eye Movement
4) Who wrote 'The Jungle Book'?
   Rudyard Kipling
5) How many faces does a dodecahedron have?
   12
6) If something is biennial, how often does it occur?
   Every 2 years
7) What European country is known in Latin as *Hibernia*?
   Ireland
8) Who, according to the Bible, saw his wife turn to a pillar of salt?
   Lot
9) Who invented bi-focal glasses?
   Benjamin Franklin
10) What is the chemical symbol for Nickel?
    Ni

Quiz 4

Round 4

1) What country hosted the inaugural FIFA World Cup in 1930?
Uruguay

2) Winston Smith smoked Victory cigarettes in which book?
1984

3) Which singer's birth name was Katheryn Elizabeth Hudson?
Katy Perry

4) Traditionally, what gift should be given for a fiftieth wedding anniversary?
Gold

5) In the hit U.S. comedy *Malcolm in the Middle*, who played Malcolm?
Frankie Muniz

6) In what year did World War II start?
1939

7) What is the capital city of Vietnam?
Hanoi

8) In what town does Spongebob live?
Bikini Bottom

9) Which Norwegian politician's actions in Worlds War II led to his surname being a byword for collaboration?
Vidkun Quisling

10) Who painted 'Vase with 15 Sunflowers'?
Vincent Van Gogh

Quiz 4

Round 5

1) What is the chemical symbol for Mercury?
   Hg
2) What is the state capital of Arizona, USA?
   Phoenix
3) What is the name of the small pieces of wood that sit atop the stumps in cricket?
   Bails
4) In which UK city would you find The Gorbals?
   Glasgow
5) What is the capital city of Uruguay?
   Montevideo
6) Which famous revolutionary was shot dead in La Higuera, Vallegrande, Bolivia, in October 1967?
   Che Guevara
7) Who wrote the short story on which The Shawshank Redemption is based?
   Stephen King
8) Robespierre is associated with which revolution?
   The French Revolution
9) Who is the main character in William Boyd's *Solo*?
   James Bond
10) Which U.S. State was the last to join the Union?
    Hawaii

Quiz 4

Round 6

1) Which is the most populous U.S. city?
New York

2) Northern Rhodesian is now known as?
Zambia

3) Operation Barbarossa was the name for the German invasion of what country in WWII?
Russia

4) Which word, used to describe a tidal wave, has been taken into English from Japanese?
Tsunami

5) What do Argentinians call The Falkland Islands?
Malvinas

6) Who wrote 'Peter Pan'?
J.M Barrie

7) What is the name of the Israeli parliament?
The Knesset

8) What was the subtitle of the first *Lord of the Rings* movie?
The Fellowship of the Ring

9) What Latin term is used in English to mean *seize the day*?
Carpe Diem

10) In what year was the Battle of Waterloo?
1815

Quiz 4

Round 7

1) What kind of an animal was the children's character Curious George?
Monkey

2) Who created the detective 'Hercule Poirot'?
Agatha Christie

3) 'Between my finger and my thumb The squat pen rests. I'll dig with it.' - Name the Nobel Laureate.
Seamus Heaney

4) A wind instrument developed by Indigenous Australians of northern Australia, it is sometimes described as a natural wooden trumpet or drone pipe - what is it?
Didgeridoo

5) What country do the French call *Le Pays Des Galles*?
Wales

6) What was the name of the boat that Darwin sailed to Galapagos?
HMS Beagle

7) What is the name of the mystery-solving cartoon dog whose best friend is called Shaggy?
Scooby Doo

8) With which religion do we associate the great Sultan Saladin?
Islam

9) Who wrote the story that 'Walter Mitty' is based on?
James Thurber

10) Prior to the Euro, what was the currency of Greece?
Drachma

Quiz 4

Round 8

1) Which festival literally translates as *Fat Tuesday*?
Mardi Gras

2) What is James Bond's family motto?
Orbis non sufficit/The World is not Enough

3) 'He wishes for the cloths of heaven' was written by which poet?
W.B. Yeats

4) Sunni and Shia are denominations of which religion?
Islam

5) Where was Paddington Bear born?
Peru

6) What is the capital city of Turkey?
Ankara

7) "Once upon a time there were three little girls who went to the police academy..." is the opening line from which TV show's Theme song?
Charlie's Angels

8) Who wrote the political philosophy entitled *The Prince*?
Niccolò Machiavelli

9) Which monarch was the intended victim of the Gunpowder Plot of 1605?
James I

10) What is the capital city of Philippines?
Manila

Quiz 4

Round 9

1) What is the capital city of Iraq?
   Baghdad
2) What was the name of Ricky Gervais' character in *The Office*?
   David Brent
3) Which character regularly died in most episodes in the early seasons of South Park?
   Kenny
4) What is the last book of the Bible?
   Revelations
5) Which Italian explorer finally returned home in 1295, having wandered Asia with his father and his uncle for 24 years?
   Marco Polo
6) Which is chronologically the first of the four Grand Slam tennis tournaments, taking place in the last fortnight of January?
   Australian Open
7) For what international cricket team did Don Bradman play?
   Australia
8) Which President of the US was indicted during the Watergate scandal?
   Richard Nixon
9) 'The Rime of the Ancient Mariner' - Name the poet who wrote this masterpiece.
   Samuel Taylor Coleridge
10) In Star Wars, what was C3PO?
    A robot

Quiz 4

Round 10

1) Which team has won the most number of NBA finals?
Boston Celtics

2) Who captained the English cricket team that infamously toured Australia in 1932/33 in what was called The Bodyline Series?   Douglas Jardine

3) In maths, what letter is used to represent the square root of -1?
i

4) In Television technology, what does LED stand for?
Light Emitting Diode

5) *Krav Maga* is a self-defence technique associated with which country?
Israel

6) What is the longest river in Italy?
Po

7) What is the name of the oven used to fire pottery?
Kiln

8) Normally, what flavour are the drinks Pastis, Sambuca and Ouzo?
Anise/Aniseed

9) In cricket, what is the term for a lower-order batsman who comes in to bat higher up the order than usual near the end of the day's play?
Night Watchman

10) Which Irish-born actor succeeded Richard Harris in the role of Dumbledore?
Michael Gambon

Quiz 5

Round 1

1) In soccer, what does the first 'F' in FIFA stand for?
   Fédération

2) Which country, founded by The American Colonisation Society in 1821, declared independence in 1847?
   Liberia

3) What is the formal name for the collar bone, in the human skeleton?
   Clavicle

4) What is the capital city of Bosnia and Herzegovina?
   Sarajevo

5) Which U.S. state's capital is Salem?
   Oregon

6) Which country's flag is Ireland's flag in reverse?
   Ivory Coast

7) What is the name of the French game, played over gravel, where a large ball is thrown so as to land as close as possible to a smaller ball?
   Boules or Pétanque

8) The NBA Basketball team - the <blank> Jazz. Fill in the blank…
   Utah

9) In what year was the Magna Carta signed?
   1215

10) What is the state capital of Arkansas, USA?
    Little Rock

Quiz 5

Round 2

1) What does the 'E' in UNICEF stand for?
Emergency

2) This city was once known as Petrograd and then Leningrad but what is it called now?
St. Petersburg

3) Which writer's birth name was Eric Arthur Blair?
George Orwell

4) One of the Seven Wonders of the Ancient World, what was the name of the giant statue that bestrode the harbour at Rhodes?
Colossus

5) In what year was the Battle of Hastings?
1066

6) What colour do you get if you mix red and yellow?
Orange

7) Which mountain range is known as *The Backbone of Italy*?
The Appenines

8) While Armstrong and Aldrin walked on the moon, who stayed behind in the capsule?
Michael Collins

9) Who painted 'The Scream'?
Edvard Munch

10) Which monarch ruled Britain from 1837 to 1901?
Queen Victoria

Quiz 5

Round 3

1) In the atom, what are the neutral particles called?
Neutrons

2) In the internet, what does URL stand for?
Uniform Resource Locator

3) Chester Carlson invented which piece of office equipment?
Photocopier

4) Who was the captain of The Bounty before the mutiny?
Captain Bligh

5) In the U.S. version of The Office, who played Michael Scott, Regional Manager of Dunder Mifflin?
Steve Carell

6) Who discovered penicillin?
Alexander Fleming

7) What drink is normally poured over Crèpe Suzette and ignited?
Grand Marnier or orange Curaçao liqueur

8) In Roman Numerals, what does MM mean?
2000

9) Which Mediterranean island was home to the Minoan civilisation?
Crete

10) In the *Lord of the Rings* films, who plays Gandalf?
Ian McKellen

Quiz 5

Round 4

1) How is acetylsalicylic acid better known?
Aspirin

2) Who was the U.S. President at the outbreak of WWII?
Franklin D. Roosevelt

3) Which British-Jamaican Rastafarian writer and poet's middle names are 'Obadiah Iqbal'?
Benjamin Zephaniah

4) In literature, who is the housekeeper at 221b Baker Street?
Mrs. Hudson

5) What is the capital city of North Korea?
Pyongyang

6) What is the name of Spongebob's starfish friend?
Patrick

7) How many cents in a nickel?
5

8) In Lawn Bowls, what is the name of the small target ball?
Jack or Kitty

9) What is the common name for the *Aurora Borealis*?
Northern Lights

10) Which MLB baseball team is based in Wrigley Field?
Chicago Cubs

Quiz 5

Round 5

1) In Roman Numerals, what does D mean?
500

2) If something is described as ovine, then what is it like?
Sheep

3) Which is the only Great Lake entirely within the U.S.?
Lake Michigan

4) From which flower do we get saffron?
Crocus

5) Who painted 'Ceci n'est pas une pipe'?
Henri Magritte

6) In medicine, how do we normally refer to the tubercle bacillus?
TB

7) What fruit are Valencia, Jaffa and Joppa types of?
Orange

8) What year did the Korean War end?
1953

9) Who was U.S. President on the 1st of January 2000?
Bill Clinton

10) What is the chemical symbol for Sulphur?
S

Quiz 5

Round 6

1) Which star of the hit comedy *How I met Your Mother* first came to our attention as Doogie Howser M.D.?
Neil Patrick Harris

2) What is the capital city of Haiti?
Port-au-Prince

3) In which European city would you find The Little Mermaid?
Copenhagan

4) What country has the internet domain '.va'?
Vatican City

5) What is the capital city of Syria?
Damascus

6) What was the name of the semi-autonomous, Nazi puppet government of France in WWII?
The Vichy Government

7) What is the area of Africa once known as Nyasaland now known as?
Malawi

8) What are the only team outside of the U.S. to have won a MLB World Series?
Toronto Bluejays

9) Prior to the Euro, what was the currency of Belgium?
Franc

10) Which Emperor died on Saint Helena in 1821?
Napoleon Bonaparte (Napoleon I)

Quiz 5

Round 7

1) Which Afrikaans word, literally meaning 'separateness' is used to describe a policy of racial segregation?
Apartheid

2) Lincoln, Washington, Roosevelt - which President is missing from the Mount Rushmore four?
Thomas Jefferson

3) Which country gifted The Statue of Liberty to the USA?
France

4) Which mythical twins, raised by a wolf, supposedly founded ancient Rome?
Romulus and Remus

5) Which inventor was known as The Wizard of Menlo Park?
Thomas Edison

6) In Hamlet, fill in the blank: "There are more things in heaven and earth, <blank>, than are dreamt of in your philosophy...
Horatio

7) If a dish is described as florentine, what vegetable must it contain?
Spinach

8) Which musician's birth name was Richard Starkey?
Ringo Starr

9) In darts, what is the largest score that can be achieved with one dart?
60

10) Who succeeded Julius Caesar as Roman Emperor?
Augustus

Quiz 5

Round 8

1) NaCl, Sodium Chloride, is better known as what?
   Salt
2) In astrology which sign is represented by a ram?
   Aries
3) What chemical has the symbol Fe?
   Iron
4) What is Carnophobia a fear of?
   Meat
5) In astrology which sign is represented by a goat?
   Capricorn
6) In the TV series House, what was Dr. House's first name?
   Gregory
7) Sveyn Forkbeard ruled which European country from 1013-1014, having usurped Ethelred the Unready?
   England
8) Of what University is Trinity College Dublin the sole college?
   University of Dublin
9) Prior to the Euro, what was the currency of Monaco?
   Franc
10) In the TV series Homeland, who played CIA agent Carrie Mathison?
   Claire Danes

Quiz 5

Round 9

1) In Roman Numerals, what does M mean?
1000
2) Who composed *Rhapsody in Blue*?
George Gershwin
3) What is the capital city of Austria?
Vienna
4) Which Dickens book features a character called Pip?
Great Expectations
5) When the Channel Tunnel was opened, the ceremony was overseen by President Mitterrand for France and but who represented England?
The Queen
6) What is the longest river in France?
Loire
7) In Greek and Roman Mythology, what was the name of the 3-headed hellhound?
Cerberus
8) In what year was the Great Fire of London?
1666
9) From what country do we get a dish called *tartiflette*?
France
10) What is the square-root of 144?
12

Quiz 5

Round 10

1) What is the state capital of Colorado, USA?
Denver

2) In Japan, what is *wasabi*?
Horseradish condiment

3) Who was U.K. Prime Minister on the 1st of January 2000?
Tony Blair

4) Who won Best Actor in the 2012 Oscars for *Lincoln*?
Daniel Day-Lewis

5) What is the capital city of Colombia?
Bogota

6) In which book might you spend a *malenky bit of cutter*?
A Clockwork Orange

7) Thompson Seedless and Zante Black Corinth are types of what?
Grape

8) A Russian folk stringed musical instrument with a characteristic triangular body and three strings - what is it?
Balalaika

9) Who was the Bond villain in *Moonraker*?
Drax

10) What is the capital city of Egypt?
Cairo

Tie-breakers

1) Who is the Roman god of the sea?
Neptune

2) Which country is also known as 'The Land of the Rising Sun'?
Japan

3) What sort of sea-creature is a Portugese Man-of-War?
Jellyfish

4) Who wrote 'Death in Venice'?
Thomas Mann

5) What is Southern Rhodesia now known as?
Zimbabwe

6) What country has the internet domain '.au'?
Australia

7) According to Greek legend, what creature dwelt at the centre of the Cretan Labyrinth?
Minotaur

8) Who wrote 'Portrait of Dorian Grey'?
Oscar Wilde

9) In chemistry, organic compounds always contain which element?
Carbon

10) In the comedy series *The Big Bang Theory*, what is Howard's surname?
Wolowitz

11) In Television technology, what does CRT stand for?
Cathode Ray Tube

12) Who invented dynamite?
Alfred Nobel

13) The Humerus, Ulna and what are the three bones in the human arm?
Radius

14) Guy Pierce played a teacher in which Australian soap opera?
Neighbours

15) Which U.S. state is nicknamed 'The Garden State'?
New Jersey

16) Which English soap takes place in Weatherfield?
Coronation Street

17) What is the capital city of Cuba?
Havana

18) Which saint's day falls on the 6th of December?
St. Nicholas

19) Which actor's birth name was Maurice Micklewhite?
Michael Caine

20) In The Simpsons, what instrument does Lisa play?
The Saxophone.

Also Available from Pillar International Publishing

By Mark Lloyd:

The Clever Kid's Quiz and Puzzle Book

The Cleverer Kid's Ready-Made Quiz Vol 1&2

The Ready-Made Kids Quiz Vol 1&2

By Jack Lloyd and Aideen O'Kelly

Detective!: A Kids' Quiz Game

By Rhys Hughes

The Young Dictator

By Rebecca Lloyd

Oothangbart: A Subversive Fable for Adults and Bears

Books available on Amazon.com

and

in all decent bookshops

The Cleverer Kid's Ready-Made Quiz

Volume 2

Compiled by Mark Lloyd

Published By
Pillar International Publishing Ltd
www.IndiePillar.com

Originally published in 2014 as part of
"The Ready-Made Schools Quiz"

Book and Cover Design by Lotte Bender

ISBN 978-1-911303-08-4

Dedication

For Lesley and Gerry

.